The Begatting of a President

Myron Roberts, Lincoln Haynes, and Sasha Gilien

drawings by Sandy Huffaker

BALLANTINE BOOKS • NEW YORK

Copyright © 1969 by Myron Roberts, Lincoln Haynes, and Sasha Gilien

All rights reserved.

This edition published by arrangement with The Vulgate Press.

First Printing: September, 1969

Printed in the United States of America

Ballantine Books, Inc.
101 Fifth Avenue, New York, New York 10003

Contents

The First Epistle of Richard to THE AMERICANS, or The Apocrypha	9
The Raising of Richard	15
L. B. Jenesis	19
The Defoliation of Eden	23
Burn, Pharoah, Burn	31
The Pacification of Goliath	36
Paradise Bossed	42
The Book of Hubert	46
Wallace Fit the Battle of Jericho	51
The Ascension	56

*To all the money changers
down at the temple*

And it came to pass that FDR begat Truman. And Truman begat Ike. And Ike begat JFK. And JFK begat LBJ. And all this was done that it might be fulfilled the prophecy which sayeth, "A little child shall be born in a grocery store in Whittier, and he shall sit upon the throne, and his administration shall be established greatly."

Now in those days the nation was sore divided and there were wars and rumors of wars, and dissenters went about the streets, and it was a weary land. When lo! there appeared unto the people three shining angels of light; Huntley, Brinkley and Cronkite in full color. And they said, "Fear not, for behold, we bring ye good tidings of great joy; for unto you is inaugurated this day in the City of Washington a Savior which is Richard the President . . ."

Now the begatting of Richard Nixon was on this wise. . . .

*The First Epistle
of Richard
to* THE AMERICANS
or
The Apocrypha

Now the Lord God planted a garden East of Whittier in a place called Yorba Linda, and out of the ground he made to grow orange trees that were good for food and the fruits thereof he labeled SUNKIST. And there grew the child Richard to manhood, and he was righteous, and he took to wife the damsel Pat, and she was righteous, and they were righteous together. For they knew not wine nor strong drink, and their status was middle-middle and they offended not. And the number of their cavities were fewer, yea forty-three percent, and they suffered not Irregularity. For they were chosen among all men.

And one day a deep sleep fell upon Richard and there appeared an Angel of the Lord which said unto him:

"Fear not, O Richard, because of thy good works,

Thy fame shall be as ketchup poured over cottage cheese,

For yea though thy beard be black, thou art comely

And thy two jowls shall be as young roes

Skipping across the tube.

Whence came it that young Richard was filled with the holy spirit of ambition, for he was a low potential, high achiever, and he tried harder that he might be Number One.

And there went out a decree from Caesar that all the world should be taxed. And the elders asked, "Who shall be our champion that we may be saved from the scourge of the New Dealers?" And they writ a classified ad upon the tablets, saying:

"Wanted: Future King of Israel. Pigmentation must not be unseemly; neither shall he partake of the Feast of unleavened bread." (For they were not equal opportunity employers.)

Whence came young Richard and he sayeth, "Yea verily I shall sweep the liberals before me and sting the Democrats with a swarm of WASPS."

And they found his words gracious and sent him to the wicked city of Washington. And he went into the Temples and drove out the Big Spenders.

And unto the sons of the New Deal he said, "Miserable sinners are ye all, wherefore shall the Un-Israel Activities Committee subpoenae ye." And he parted the Red Sea. And his enemies hissed and crieth, "Deliver us from Tricky Dick," and asked, "Wouldst buy a used chariot from this man?"

Now it came to pass that Ike ruled over Israel and he summoned young Richard unto him saying, "Art thou clean as a hound's tooth?" And Richard went on TV and cried, "I am clean, I am innocent and my wife weareth a Republican cloth coat." Wherefore did Richard sit at Ike's right hand and it was a time of peace. And the people went unto tracts of houses crying, "Yea verily I am a veteran and the down is low." And the voice of the escrow was heard in the land.

And the time that Ike ruled over Israel was eight years and he grew old, wherefore he chose Nixon to reign in his stead, saying, "Kings are not always wise; sometimes they are just there." And Nixon journeyed unto the land of the Latins but they liked him not and spat upon him. And he journeyed to the land of the false prophet Marx, and he went into their kitchens and spat in their borsht. But when he returned the people muttered, "Is he not overmuch righteous? For the proud die young, and he that liveth by the Bomb shall perish by it."

And there rose up against him a young prophet John, of the tribe of Joseph, a man of many talents and leader of a mighty clan. And he took Nixon by his beard and broadcast him down. And Richard's heart grew sad and he walked through the Valley of The Shadow of The Losers. Whence did he hie back unto California where he strove to be chief. But he was beaten by the jawbone of an ass. And when the scribes came unto him, he said:

"Yea I asked for votes and ye gave me the shaft. Woe unto ye, for ye shall not have Nixon to smite around anymore."

And Richard departed alone. And the liberals laughed and mocked him. And he gat no heat and he died. And he was four years dead.

The Raising of Richard

Now it came to pass that the Republicans saw there was confusion amongst their enemies and the new election would fall upon them. And they asked, "But who is there to lead us that we may cast out the Democrats and dwell in the tents of power?" And they searched their hearts.

Some amongst them cried out for Romney the Rambler. But the chieftains beheld him and saw that his brain had been washed. And others cried out for Rockefeller, for lo! His name ringeth of bullion. But the chiefs regarded him and found a taint, for he had drunk not from the cup of Gold Water. And there was Ronald, he of the late, late show, whose hair, like his heart, was dyed black. And the South clave unto him, but the delegates cast him forth, for he was not the hero but the hero's best friend.

Wherefore they cried out, "Could we but raise Richard from the dead, we should have a mighty champion and slayer of Democrats." And the Republicans said unto themselves, "We are the Resurrection and the Life, and the Law and the Order. He that believeth in us, though he were dead, yet shall he live."

But the supporters of Rocky cried out, "He hath lain four years in his grave, wherefore he stinketh."

And the Republicans said, "Yet shall we raise him, and he shall be perfumed o'er and anointed

with moderation, that he may become a New Nixon."

And they said unto him, "Richard, rise and come forth." And lo! He came forth bound hand and foot with winding sheets. And they took them from him and brought him a New Image.

And they said, "The first Nixon was of the Earth; the last is of the Spirit." And the Spirit of God lighted upon him like a Dove.

And he said, "I came back. For he that loseth the election shall win it, and the last shall be first. But is it not meet that I should have a running mate?" And they brought him an Agnew, and together they journeyed forth across the land, like unto living men.

L. B. Jenesis

In the beginning LBJ created the Great Society.

And darkness was upon the face of the Republicans. And the spirit of consensus moved across the land. And LBJ said, "Let us continyuh," and they continued. And the evening and the morning were the first day.

And LBJ said, "Let us make war on poverty," and, lo, there were welfare checks fallen upon the

land, and upon them it was writ, "Fold not, neither shall ye spindle nor multilate."

And LBJ saw that it was good. And the evening and the morning were the second day.

And LBJ said, "Let there be a Civil Rights Covenant to unite the children of light and darkness."

And so it came to pass the Congress. And the evening and the morning were the third day.

And LBJ said, "Let there be Medicare, that the sick may be healed and the doctors paid unto the fullest measure thereof."

And LBJ saw that it was paid. And the evening and the morning were the fourth day.

And LBJ said, "Let there be bureaus and departments without number, and let them be fruitful and multiply, so that every critter that flieth, creepeth or voteth shall be blessed with patronage, each in his own precinct."

And LBJ saw that it was finger-lickin' good. And the evening and the morning were the fifth day.

And LBJ said, "Let there be nuclear nonproliferation, and let the capitalist lie down with the commissar, that they may exchange corn and culture."

And LBJ pulled out his poll and saw that it was good, even unto the tenth cubit. And the evening and the morning were the sixth day.

And LBJ saw the Society that he had made, and, behold, it was Great. And on the seventh day he gave a barbecue.

Still LBJ rested not from his labors but said, "Shucks, let there be an eighth day." And on the eighth day he escalated.

The Defoliation of Eden

And LBJ said, "Let us make a voter in our image, that he may glorify us and elect us forever." And he had it made.

Then LBJ said, "It is not meet that man should vote alone." So he caused a deep sleep to fall upon the man, while his eyes grew heavy with the Late Show, and he took one of the ribs from his TV Dinner and from it he fashioned a woman, and he called their names Adam and Eve.

And they were both registered Democrats, and they were not ashamed.

And he gave unto them dominion over 2.2 children and a house in the suburbs in a tract which he called Eden Estates. And he commanded Adam that he should sustain Eve with the fruits of the shopping center, that the economy might flourish.

And LBJ said unto Adam and Eve, "Of every fruit of the Great Society save one may ye eat. But of the fruit of dissent ye shall not eat, for on that day ye shall surely doubt. Wherefore ye may not tune the tube unto the forbidden channel of Full Bright, nor seek to understand the accursed Code of Morse."

Wherefore did they gather them before the tube, for truly that was the Light of the World. And Adam rested beside his six-pack and beheld the eternal cowherds beset by the feathered tribes of Geronimo.

But a heaviness of spirit came over Eve, and, lo, she was bored. Wherefore did she flick the dial, and there was a flurry of snow and pestilential advertising, and it came upon three handmaidens with their miniskirts raised north of Jericho, and a youth who sought to cleave unto them, and it was called the Mating Game. And unto the chosen one was given a journey to the wicked city of the Vegasites, 600 shekels of silver and a set of matched luggage.

But unto Eve this, too, was an abomination and a drag.

Now did Adam drift off to the land of Nod, and there entered into Eden Estates an Intellectual, who was more subtile than any serpent, and he said unto the woman, "Thou mayest indeed tune unto the forbidden channel and see it like it is, baby."

And, lo, she beheld a flash of light, and great speckled birds from the sky hurling bolts of flame upon the hamlets of the followers of the bearded prophet Ho. And the dread hordes of the Congniks in their pajamas of one color—black—descended in their wrath upon the palaces of the Chosen, and there was a great battle. And its name was Tet, and it was offensive.

Now when Eve beheld this she was sore afraid and cried out, so that Adam awakened. And he said, "What manner of channel beholdest thou? This scene is forbidden, and for this disobedience LBJ shall surely smite thee."

But in her pride Eve answered, "Stupid, thy brain hath been washed. Remove the veil from thine eyes."

Wherefore did Adam look. And the scene changed to the Chambers of the Senators, and it was Full Bright who did speak like unto a dove.

"There are wars and rumors of wars," spake the wise one, "but the truth is more precious and more rare than Myrrh and Frankincense D. Roosevelt . . .

This war profiteth ye not, nor doth it succor the sons of Asia. Therefore escalate not, lest ye be escalated."

Whereupon did the heavens thunder, and there was a flash of lightning and a mighty blast of the Texas longhorn, and lo! The Omnipotent One appeared, surrounded by his host of Cherubim. And foremost amongst these was the angel Rusk, who said, "Ye shall honor your commitments before the SEATO of the Mighty all the rest of your days."

And there was the mighty warrior Wastemoreland, who doth search much but destroyeth little, and the Archangel Hubert, who had been exalted above all men, that he might sing hosannas and deliver the liberals unto the Most High.

And unto Adam and Eve spake LBJ, "Who first seduced you into this foul revolt?"

Whereupon did Eve cry out, "The Intellectual—he it was who turned me on."

Then did LBJ say unto the Intellectual, "Because thou hast done this thing, thou art accursed, and thy head shall be of egg. The FBI shall set a watch upon thee, and trouble shall plague thee all the days of thy tenure; for renewal of thy grants, upon thy belly shalt thou crawl."

And unto Adam and Eve he said, "Because ye have been disobedient and hearkened unto the dissenter, a surtax shall be laid upon you, inflation shall be visited upon your heads, and your stocks and bonds shall be brought low."

Therefore did LBJ banish them east of Eden Estates, and they wandered in desolation until they came to a place called Credibility Gap.

Burn, Pharaoh, Burn

Now the sons of Adam were fruitful, and there was affluence in the land. But among the children of the Great Society there were those whose skins were black. And lo! Their portion was niggardly, and of the fatted calf they were left sucking hind teat.

And they were the pickers of cotton and shiners of shoes, for, in the words of the white psalmist, they had plenty of nothin' and nothin' was plenty for them. And it was decreed that they should sit apart from the seats of the mighty, yea, even unto the restrooms.

Now it came to pass that a prophet rose up amongst them, and they called him King. And he went unto Pharaoh and said, "Let my people go to the front of the bus."

But Pharaoh answered: "In the fullness of time and with all deliberate speed shall this thing come to pass. When ye shall prove yourselves worthy, shall ye have your just portion—yea, verily, like unto a snowball in Hell."

Wherefore King assembled a great host, and he led them unto the lunch counters of the land, and he asked for bread, and they gave him a stone in the head. And he was set upon by fierce dogs, which are the Man's best friend.

Now the avenging angel Carmichael cried out, "Give me some men who are black-hearted men.

For ours is the kingdom and the glory and the black power."

And the young men girded up their loins and filled their Coke bottles with Platformate, for quicker starts, and there were burnt offerings in the streets.

And the summer waxed long and hot, and it was the Molotov cocktail hour. And there was a gnashing of teeth and smashing of windows, and the people descended upon the merchants, and lo! There was instant credit.

And the Man was wroth, and he smote them with the back of his lash.

Then the King spake, "Render unto Sears the things that are Sears', for what profiteth it a man to gain a colored television set and lose his soul, brother?"

And the King journeyed to the city of Memphis,

and he spake unto the collectors of offal, and he said, "Ye shall overcome."

But an assassin rose up against him, and he slew the King. And there were wailings and lamentations in the land.

The Pacification of Goliath

For lo! The winter was passing, and the stickers were brought forth abundantly on the bumpers, and the voice of the candidate was heard in the land. Then the Democrats gathered together their armies to battle at New Hampshire. And the regulars stood on a mountain on the right side, and the dissenters stood on a mountain on the left side, and between was the valley of the Generation Gap.

Now there came out of Washington the champion of the regulars, LBJ, whose height was six cubits and a span. In his right arm was a mighty staff of brass, and in his left, shekels without number. And when he spake the young men trembled, for there was a mighty draft.

And he stood and cried out to the armies of the dissenters, "Wherefore come ye forth to challenge me? Am I not your chieftain, and are ye not servants of the party? Have I not brought you blessings without number? Ye have never had it so good. Sons of dissent, ye are an abomination and a passel of no-good hippies, and a stench in the nostrils of the nation."

Then the dissenters spake out, "Hypocrite! Thou criest peace, peace, but there is no peace. The words of thy mouth are as honey, but thy deeds as gall. And thou goest in stiff-necked pride, wherefore are our sons sacrificed that thou mayest play Texas Ranger to the world."

But still no man in their ranks had heart to go forth and battle the giant LBJ.

Then it came to pass that there rose among them a shepherd from the hills of Minnesota who was called Eugene. And he cried out, "Who is this uncircumcised Philistine, that he should mock the young liberals? I shall smite him in the primaries and deliver you from his hand, and the little children shall lead me."

And the scribes mocked him, saying, "Precinct captains hast thou none, nor talents of silver. Lucky thou art to deliver thine own state."

But Eugene took up his sling and drew near to the giant, who disdained him and said, "Thinkest that I fear thy sling? Surely thou knowest I am the mightiest slinger of them all."

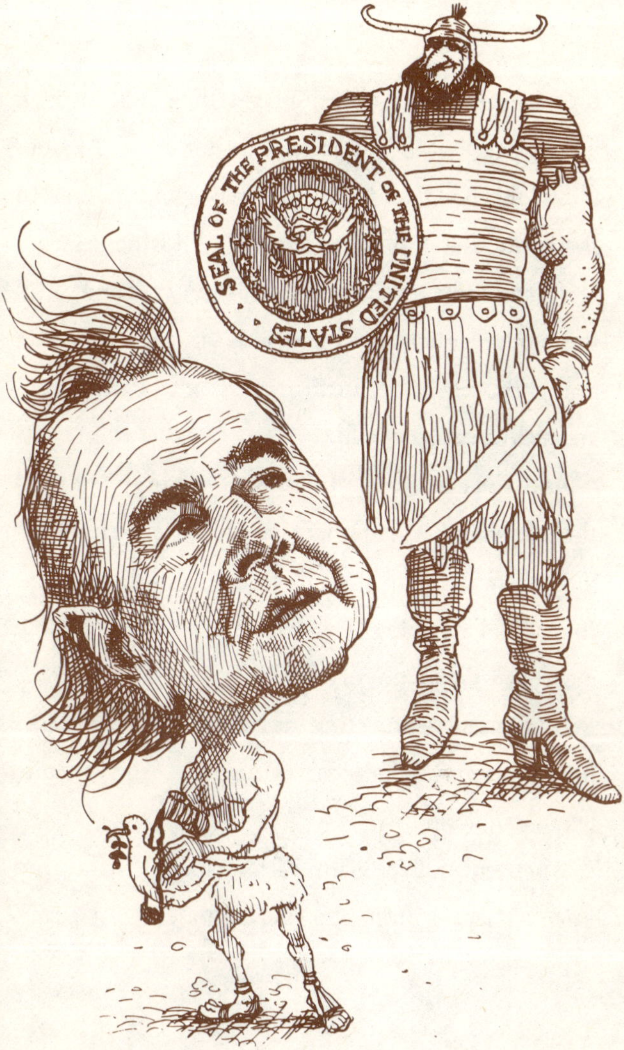
SEAL OF THE PRESIDENT OF THE UNITED STATES

But Eugene feared not. Then it was that he took up the peace vote and slang it, and it smote LBJ between the polls, and the giant fell upon his face to the earth, and the land trembled. And the regulars were sore amazed, and they turned and fled. And the dissenters rose and shouted, "Eugene, thou art a mighty candidate. Lead us now into convention, and deliver us from evil."

And Eugene, in the fullness of victory, accepted their homage, when there suddenly appeared before them Bobby, son of Joseph and brother of John. And he said, "Lo, I have reassessed. Follow me, that we may go forward."

And many among the people reached to touch his raiment and the locks of his hair. And he, too, was a candidate.

Then the fallen giant LBJ raised his head and said, "There is a time for war and a time for peace, a time to run and a time to split. Wherefore shall I offer peace to the sons of Ho and return unto the Banks of Pedernales, and deposit therein."

Paradise Bossed

Now Bobby was a hairy man. He was the son of many-shekeled Joseph and brother of John, who was King of Kings. And many sons and daughters were given unto him, for he was fruitful and multiplied past all understanding.

Whilst but a youth he rose up in righteousness and smote the Hoffa-ite king of the charioteers. Many sons of Ham and eggheads sought out Bobby to hear the wisdom which God had put into his heart, and he stood up beautiful before all men.

Then it came to pass that John was foully slain, and thrones were cast down, and there was a falling off. And Bobby's place at the Lord's right hand was taken by the Archangel Hubert, whose mouth was full of tongue. And there were murmurings of discontent amongst the people.

Wherefore did LBJ summon Bobby unto him and say, "Art thou he that troubleth my reign and sacrificeth not unto me?"

And Bobby answered him, "I have troubled not thy reign, but thou, usurper-king in my brother's house, hast gone whoring after the generals. Thou hast impoverished the spirit, and where once stood Pablo Casals thou bringest in Martha Raye."

Then did LBJ command, "Get thee hence and show not thy face in my councils, lest I cast thee into a barbecue pit of fire and brimstone. And take thine accursed eggheads with thee."

Wherefore did Bobby gather his brethren and

go forth into exile—yea, even unto the farthest reaches of Hell's Kitchen. And at his side was Galbraith, apostle of affluence, whose thoughts, like his bulk, towered o'er all men; and there also went Schlesinger the scribe, and Sorensen the Holy Ghost, and sundry sons of Harvard, thinkers all and builders of the Lofty Premise.

And Bobby summoned his councillors and said, "Soon there shall come the election. Shall it fall on me? Shall we take arms against this sea of Texans and by opposing end them?"

But the councillors replied, "Strive not with this mighty man, lest he take thee by thy forelock, and he will surely shear thee like a sheep. Let not thy strength be wasted. Why shouldst thou die before thy time? Keep thy counsel and observe the opportunity."

And Bobby hearkened unto them, for he knew that it was writ, "Ye can't smite City Hall."

But then Bobby's heart was moved and he entered the fray. And lo! The people enlisted under his banner and cried out, "O Bobby, brother of Jack, lead us out of this wilderness lest we perish." And he went into the primaries and the states gave way before his mighty host. And he came unto a place called California where he strove mightily with his foes. And he was victorious. And then a foul assassin, a son of Ishmael, rose up against him and he was slain, and strong men wept and the people were sore afraid and the houses were in mourning and the daughters of Jerusalem were brought low. For those who had seen a great light saw only darkness now, and they sat upon the ground and wept.

The Book of Hubert

There was a man in the land of US whose name was Hubert; and that man was perfect and upright, and one that feared LBJ and eschewed dissent. In the days of his youth he had known liberalism, and when the liberals came not unto the house of LBJ and cursed him in their hearts, Hubert sinned not, nor charged LBJ foolishly.

Thus said Hubert continually, "Naked came I out of the Senate and naked shall I return, ere I

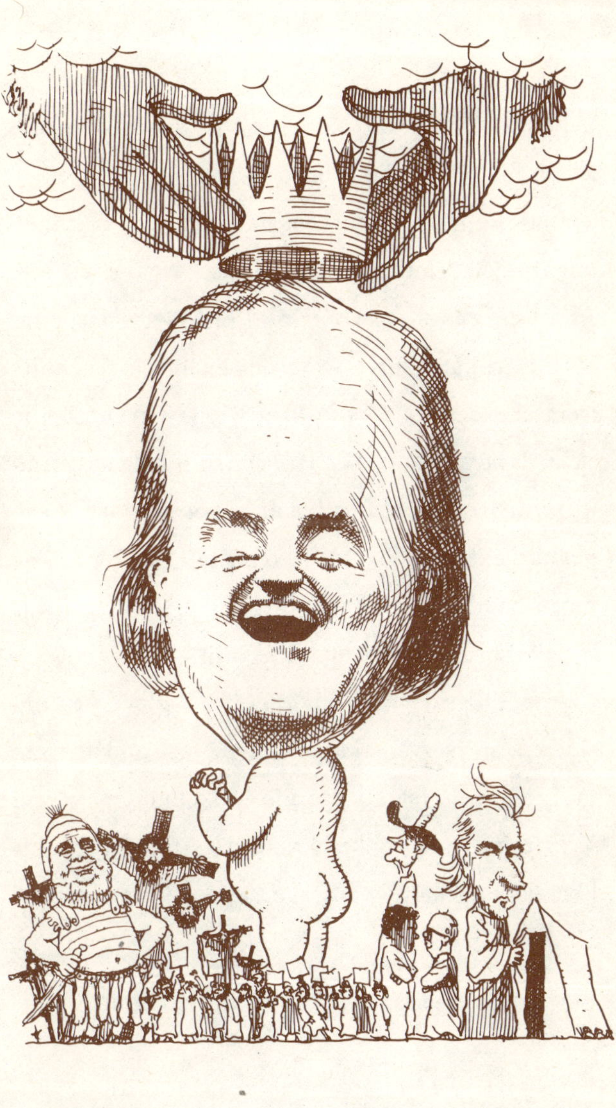

defy my Maker. For LBJ giveth and LBJ taketh away. Blessed be the name of Texas."

And the Democrats went unto Chicago that they might rejoice and take unto themselves a new King. And they came everyone from his own place. And in this congregation were Jesse and his cohorts from the deserts of the West, followers unto the slain Bobby, whose hearts were sore afflicted. And there was Julian of Bond, and Lester, wielder of the mighty axe-handle. And Connally, boss unto the ranch-hands. And foremost amongst them was Daley, Lord of Hosts and Maker of Kings.

And LBJ said unto his captains, "Have ye considered my servant Hubert, a perfect and upright man, one who feareth me and walketh in my ways? Yea, though he talketh with the tongue of the liberals, he shall not forsake me, for his supporters are few and full of Labor."

And when the people heard that the election should fall upon Hubert they were dismayed and rushed into the streets shouting, "Should not the multitude of lies be answered? Should a man full of talk be justified?"

And the Hippites and the Yippites and the followers of Eugene came forth and jeered. Wherefore did Daley summon unto him his hosts and say unto them, "Let us welcome these children unto Chicago; let us lay out a carpet of red. Let us silence this bleating of the sheep. Smite them and deliver them unto my hand."

And they smote the children of Israel. But there stood a watchman on the tower and his name was Walter the Cronkite, and he cried out against the slaughter of the innocents.

Wherefore did Hubert win the nomination, but it was as dust and ashes in his mouth. And his words were as sounding brass and a tinkling cymbal. And he was covered with boils. And the followers of Eugene cried unto him, "Thou has lost thine integrity. Go worship LBJ and be damned."

And damned if he wasn't.

Wallace Fit the Battle of Jericho

Now in the midst of Israel there was a mighty college and it was called Jericho U. And therein dwelt those of the long hair. Whilst other men labored with the sweat of their brow so that their necks grew red beneath the sun, those of Jericho gave themselves over to disputation and dissipation. Now when the Israelites went forth to make war against the Congniks, the young men of Jericho fought not, neither did they report for induction. And they marched forth into the cities and caused great tumult therein. And they made burnt offerings of their draft cards, and they mocked the elders of Zion. Their noise was famed throughout Israel. And the people cursed them, crying out, "O ye shameless, hairy, unwashed sinners, ye are abomination."

And it came to pass that a man arose from South of Eden, and he was called Josh Wallace, he who had stood at the gate of The Great Temple of 'Bama and shouted, "If ye are black, git ye back." And he said, "Of the Lord am I now come to rid Israel of these pinks, perverts and punks, which are a pestilence upon the land." And he went into the fields and into the towns and into the suburbs and gathered together all those who despised miscegenation, integration and education. "Let us go against these rebellious sons and the proud judges of this earth and teach them that he that lieth down before our chariots shall not rise again."

And he summoned unto him a mighty warrior, Nuke LeMay. And Wallace said unto Nuke, "Wilt thou make a covenant that together we shall go unto Jericho and smite the sinners therein?" And LeMay said, "Yea verily, let us scourge them with fire, and SAC their cities that all the evil works they have done under the sun shall be vaporized in a cloud like unto a mushroom." But Josh stayed his hand, and sayeth, "It is not meet that ye speak thus before the election, for a little bird shall hear thy words and carry them unto the media and the people will fear us."

And they gathered together a mighty host and the people saw them and cried out, "Look, a white tornado hath come to cleanse the land!" And they marched around Jericho U. seven times, but the walls were stout and the bearded ones therein de-

54

fiant. Then Wallace gathered his police together and they blew a mighty blast on their bullhorns and the walls came tumbling down. And they burnt the city and there was a great Dixie Fry.

The Ascension

Now Nixon came unto the people and lifted his arms high and showed them the palms of his hands, that they might see the marks of his Crucifixion and marvel at his Resurrection. And the people were sore amazed. And he cried out to them, "Behold the man: Nixon's the One, and I am the Re-election and the Right." But they regarded him as Richard the Lyin' Hearted, and but a Fisher of Votes, and they believed him not.

But Richard said unto them, "Verily, when I was young I girded up my loins and smeared with a mighty hand. And mine enemies cried out against me and said, 'Beware, beware.' Then I knew that I had sinned, and I suffered wretchedness and desolation of the spirit, and from the Electoral College I dropped out.

"But lo! I am born again. Wherefore love me. Feed my sheep and get ye unto the precincts and baptize the unbelievers in the name of the Father, the Son and the Holy Spiro."

Then it came to pass that the voters blessed him, albeit the Hump made it a tight camel race. And he was received up into Heaven and sat on the right hand of GOP. For the Republicans were in the temple praising and blessing Nixon, whereupon he spake unto the media:

"There is a time to integrate and a time to nonproliferate. It is better to give missiles than to re-

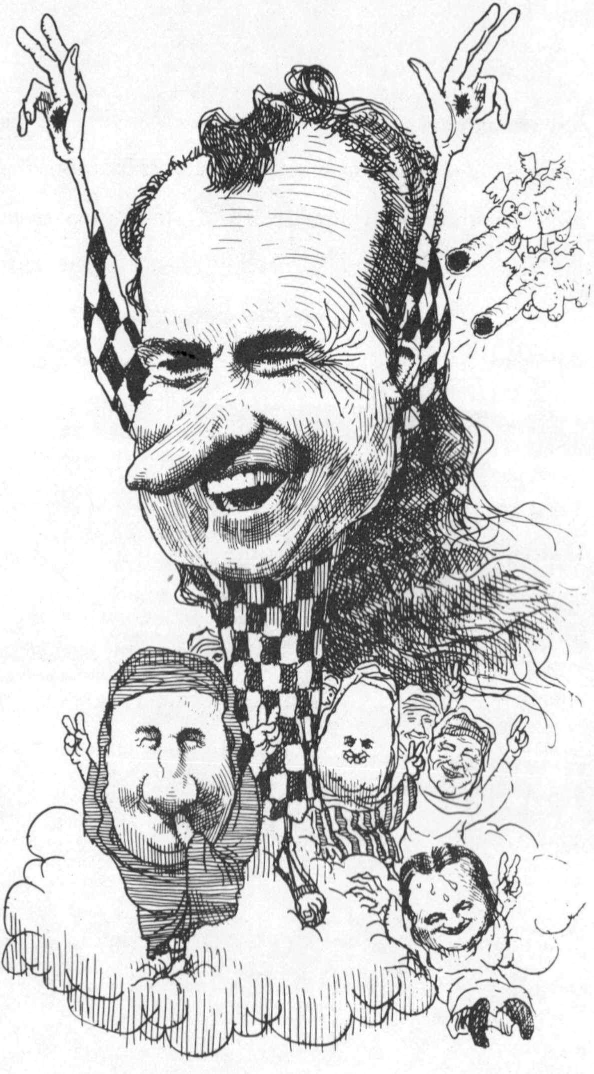

ceive them, yet shall we profit more from the Stock Exchange than a nuclear exchange. Wherefore verily I say unto ye, let us lower our voices and raise our prices. For in my White House are many millionaires, and they go to prepare a better place for ye."

And there was great rejoicing throughout the suburbs, yea, even unto Orange County.

Amen.

". . . The race is not to the swift, nor the battle to the strong, neither yet bread to the wise, nor yet riches to men of understanding, nor yet favor to men of skill; but time and chance happeneth to them all."

—Ecclesiastes